The Last Years of Steam on the

LONDON

MIDLAND

REGION

PAUL LEAVENS & SVMRC

Copyright Book Law Publications – First published in the United Kingdom in 2019

ISBN 978-1-909625-96-9

Printed and bound by The Amadeus Press, Cleckheaton, West Yorkshire

Published by Book Law Publications, 382 Carlton Hill, Nottingham, NG4 1JA

Introduction

The purpose of this album is to present various images which portray sections of the London Midland Region during the final years of steam operation. To that end we will be including the odd picture of diesel operations because the transition period from the introduction of diesel motive power to the elimination of steam was somewhat elongated and so the inevitable meetings were bound to happen.

So that some semblance of order is kept, we will be starting our pictorial journey at Carlisle Kingmoor, right on the northern border with the Scottish Region. Although Kingmoor engine shed was of Caledonian Railway origin, we had chosen the period when the motive power depot was coded 12A in the LMR listing to eliminate any doubt. We will proceed south via the West Coast main-line calling at Shap and other locations in the boundary of the Lake District. Carnforth will bring us to sea level and then it's along to Preston where we deviate west and east of the WCML for brief visits to Kirkham, Bolton and Manchester. Regaining the main line we get to Crewe where we make another short deviation to Bescot before the arrival of the motorway in those parts!

Northampton is another location off the usual path but we are soon heading south again towards London and its multitude of railway charms. We finish off with a good look around Camden, then down the bank to Euston station where we end this illustrative tour of the LMR's Western Lines.

Other parts of the Region will be covered in future volumes so we are not leaving anywhere out. Throughout the volume it will be noticed we have used the twenty-four hour clock but one or two obvious exceptions do crop up so please bear with us. Nevertheless we hope you enjoy this north to south tour and delight in the nostalgia and history as much as we have putting it all together.

David Allen, Newstead Abbey, Nottinghamshire 2019.

(cover) 'Duchess' No.46251 CITY OF NOTTINGHAM at Shrewsbury in 1963. It was usual for Crewe to send ex-works Pacifics on a running-in turn to Shrewsbury where a 70ft turntable was installed at the motive power depot for such occasions. Besides the turntable the triangular junction south of the station was a useful back-up. *PL/BLP.*

(rear cover top) Leaving the cooling towers of Willesden junction behind, Cl.5 No.45234 runs through Kensall Green in charge of an Up express circa 1962. *PL/BLP.*

(rear cover bottom) Reb. Patriot No.45530 SIR FRANK REE stables on Willesden shed in 1961. *PL/BLP.*

(above) We start our journey at Kingmoor motive power depot on 12th April 1966 with a host of Stanier Cl.5s – 44899, 45105 and 45120 identified – rubbing shoulders with BR Standards, of which 'Britannia' No.70051 is prominent. Miniature snow ploughs are still fitted to many engines as the winter lessens its grip on the land in a slow menacing way; the authorities are taking no chances! *(below)* Inside the shed, showing off their identification and place of residence are Cl.5s No.44902 and 45259. *Both PL/BLP.*

(above) Kingmoor based 'Duchess' No.46257 CITY OF SALFORD at home on Saturday 13th June 1964 with less than three months of operations before withdrawal! Also on shed that day were three unusual visitors in the shape of Southern Region 'Merchant Navy' No.35012 UNITED STATES LINES, preserved GNofSR 4-4-0 No.49 GORDON HIGHLANDER, and the Caledonian Railway 'Single' No.123; all three had been involved in special workings. *(below)* Having left 12A behind we proceed towards Carlisle (Citadel) station but beforehand we come across this busy scene at Etterby on the bridge spanning the River Eden. Identified on this date of 6th April 1966 are Ivatt 4 No.43139 working Up empties to Kingmoor yard whilst 'Brit' No.70033, and Cl.5 No.44838 are making their way independently into the city on the same track! *Both PL/BLP.*

(above) It was rare to find ex-LMS 3F 0-6-0T still shunting anywhere on the region in June 1964 but on the 13th of that month Citadel station still had one – No.47667 – as pilot. Here the 3F is just about to haul some empty stock over to Upperby carriage shed. *PL/BLP. (below)* Leeds Holbeck based 'Royal Scot' No.46109 ROYAL ENGINEER stands at the head of the Up working of *THE THAMES-CLYDE EXPRESS* in May 1961. The clock shows 1155 and the fireman is atop the tender ready to fill the water tank. Other than the three 'spotters' on the opposite platform, who don't appear too interested in proceedings, there is only the photographer who is. It was the everyday running of the railways which – admitted – we all took for granted! Luckily the photographers did not and that is why this album is dedicated to them for their foresight. Although not going our way or even to the same destination, the 7P will be working initially through London Midland territory, then the North Eastern Region followed by a stint through the Eastern Region before regaining the LMR. The train has already covered nearly a hundred miles through the Scottish Region making it one of the most cosmopolitan trains on BR. Now what about that mottled shadow effect? *BLP.*

(top) In its namesake city, 'Duchess' No.46238 CITY OF CARLISLE looks rather splendid on the shed yard at Upperby on 13th June 1964. *(above)* In the same position but some ten weeks later, sister No.46243 CITY OF LANCASTER wears the more usual garb of filth. *(left)* Inside the roundhouse on that same day, two 'Scots' in everything but name take a rest; No.46115 SCOTS GUARDSMAN and rebuilt 'Jubilee' No.45736 PHOENIX were both resident 7Ps. *All PL/BLP.*

(top) Ivatt Cl.2 No.46426 looks rather splendid in this night view inside the roundhouse on 11th April 1966. *(above)* Class leader No.46200 still has number and works plate affixed on 13th June 1964. Having been withdrawn in November 1962, the lady was now ready for whatever fate awaited. During the following September a yard in Scotland despatched the Pacific. *Both PL/BLP*.

(above) A year earlier on 11th August 1963 the shed yard at Upperby was hosting WD 2-10-0 No.90763 which was en route to a scrapyard. *(below)* On that same Sunday there was further doom and gloom as 'Jubilee' No.45640 FROBISHER and 'Crab' No.42875 share the same road awaiting the inevitable! *Both PL/BLP*.

(above) We have arrived at Shap where all of the action is northbound whereas we are southbound. No matter, we have time enough to take in the scenery besides looking at many of the trains working up and down the bank. Our first encounter is with 'Britannia' No.70035 RUDYARD KIPLING which was heading a Down express and was being banked by an unknown Class 4 tank from Tebay shed on a glorious Saturday 1st August 1964. (below) On that same Saturday these two have really got into the spirit of things and are showing the visiting enthusiasts what to expect from most Down trains, be they express passenger or lowly goods working. Carnforth Cl.4 No.42680 escorts 'Royal Scot' No.46115 SCOTS GUARDSMAN which was paying its passage to Upperby after being transferred from Longsight that very day; note the nameplate is missing but the backing plate is in situ! Both PL/BLP.

(above) After waiting for all the Up expresses to pass, BR Standard 9F No.92021, along with its lengthy goods train was allowed out onto the main line during the afternoon of Saturday 25th July 1964. The former Crosti-boilered 2-10-0 was looking as expected by this time in the Sixties with filth everywhere. The Kingmoor crew acknowledge the photographer as they head south on what was probably a spot of overtime. (below) Even the diesels used steam bankers when necessary. Working a Down express at Scout Green, Crewe North's EE Type 4 D338 had rear end assistance on 10th August 1963. Both PL/BLP.

(top) Banking wasn't always required as this northbound express proves passing Scout Green on 10th August 1963. The train engine was 'Jubilee' No.45681 ABOUKIR from Blackpool which was double-headed by Carnforth based but soon to be stablemate No.42464, a Stanier Cl.4 tank which was just about to be transferred to Blackpool from Carnforth. Both locomotives are shockingly dirty but they are in fine fettle in charge of this ten-coach load. *(centre)* Another image from 10th August 1963 with rain expected during continuous overcast. Kingmoor 'Clan' No.72009 CLAN STEWART adds to the latter but doesn't win anything in the cleaning stakes. However, photographer Paul Leavens is acknowledged by the driver sounding the whistle as the ten vehicle train complete with banker makes its way towards the summit at Shap. *(above)* We know about the Peppercorn and Thompson ex-LNER Pacifics which were allocated at Polmadie in the early Sixties and which plied the WCML south to Carlisle and apparently as far as Crewe on occasion. However, this A1, No.60131 OSPREY working an Up express at Scout Green on 1st August 1964 was a Neville Hill engine at the time it was captured on film. The train is ECML in origin but the reason for its diversion is unknown. *All PL/BLP.*

(above) Now who is working hardest? 8F No.48512 heads a Down freight at Scout Green on 17th August 1963 with banking assistance. It appears that the slower the train the harder it was to get to the summit! *(below)* In the cutting near the top of the climb, Carnforth Cl.4 No.42538 gives assistance to 'Royal Scot' No.46140 THE KING'S ROYAL RIFLE CORPS working a Down express on the 11th August 1963. *Both PL/BLP.*

(above) Scout Green again! Its Sunday 18th August 1963 and Carnforth Cl.4 tank No.42299 is putting on a good show for one and all whilst it helps Willesden Cl.5 No.45065 which has charge of this train of returning empty milk vans and tanks. Note the livestock in the adjoining field grazing with apparent nonchalance. *(below)* Another milk train but this one is loaded and going south to market. D300 whistles along the main line as it coasts down the bank with this London bound train on Wednesday 21st August 1963. *Both PL/BLP.*

(above) A last look at Shap during the summer of 1963! Newton Heath Cl.5 No.44893 double-heading an equally hard-working 'Royal Scot' No.46168 THE GIRL GUIDE of Springs Branch on 21st August 1963; the northbound express has thirteen on – mainly Mk.1s note – including a Buffet car. The locomotive combination is interesting but it was 1963 and anything could and did happen! *(below)* Whilst working a Down freight, Cl.5 No.44816 gets a push from an unidentified Stanier Cl.4 tank at Shap Wells on 3rd May 1965. *Both PL/BLP.*

(above) It is a shame the engine is dirty, and that it has no nameplate anymore but 'Brit' No.70043 formerly LORD KITCHENER (aka The Butcher) brings us one last time to the summit of Shap where the BR sign announces to all on 3rd May 1965 that the summit of the railway is 916 feet above sea level! *(below)* As quick as a flash we are down in Tebay where on Sunday 9th May 1965 a Stanier 8F along with a Stanier Cl.5 coupled to a train – sorry but both engines are unidentified – are involved with track relaying duties. The River Lune completes the tranquillity of the location. *Both PL/BLP.*

(above) We arrive in Carnforth in time to see Blackpool Cl.5 No.44947 heading south through the junction with a container train in August 1952. *(below)* 4F No.44060 arrives in Carnforth's exchange and marshalling sidings in August 1952 with a Down fitted freight. The external condition of the 0-6-0 reveals that it wasn't just during the 1960s that steam suffered from lack of cleaning. *Both SVMRC.*

(above) It is oft forgotten just how much freight used to ply the WCML. Although there were many sections where trains would join for short journeys of say less than a hundred miles, there was quite a number of them which traversed the whole length from London to Glasgow and beyond to Perth and Aberdeen. This van train running through Carnforth in August 1952 and hauled by grubby 8F No.48513 of Edge Hill shed was typical of the fitted and express freight which ran in-between the paths of the Anglo-Scottish expresses over the northern section of the main-line. *(below)* Another Liverpool based engine; Caprotti fitted Class 5 No.44743 was one of Bank Hall's allocation and was making its way south from Carnforth in August 1952. *Both SVMRC.*

(above) Fast forward to August 1960 now and local Cl.5 No.44904 draws into the goods loop with a train from Workington. (below) They had started! English Electric Type 4 D229 thunders through Carnforth along the Up main on a sunny August afternoon in 1960 with an Anglo-Scottish express. In one of those peculiarities of locomotive allocations, these 2,000 h.p. diesels were initially allocated to strategic depots along the WCML: Camden, Crewe, Longsight, Edge Hill, and Carlisle Upperby but they were never allocated to Polmadie even though that depot used to service all of the class working into Glasgow. The LMS stationed their Pacifics strategically at Camden, Crewe, Upperby and Polmadie but these diesels were treated differently! Both SVMRC.

(above) That's better! Heading a northbound express at speed through Carnforth in August 1960, 'Duchess' No.46247 CITY OF LIVERPOOL has what appears to be one of the eight-coach Anglo-Scottish expresses without a headboard. Note how the goods yard appears some eight years after 4F No.44060 ran into a rather crowded fan of sidings. To quote a line from a song that would become popular within a few years of this scene being recorded 'The times, they are a changing!' *(below)* Having put its goods train into the marshalling sidings, No.44904 makes its way to shed. The goods yard here held over a thousand wagons when fully operational but that was then! *Both SVMRC.*

(above) The back-way to Carnforth engine shed – approaching from the south – in August 1960 took engines past the coal stacks, alongside the Cripples siding and straight beneath the coaling plant. Within a decade this motive power depot would be privately owned and become a leading light in the steam locomotive preservation movement. For those of you who haven't seen a concrete mechanical coal plant in a long time the structure at Carnforth is still extant and worth a visit if you're going that way. *(below)* Locally based Stanier 5 No.45427 hauling an Up goods working, runs into Carnforth and begins to slow the train in August 1960. *Both SVMRC.*

(above) D7 INGLEBOROUGH, one of the original ten 'Peaks' waits in the goods loop at Carnforth in August 1960 for the arrival of an early afternoon passenger train from the Cumbrian coast which it will haul to a destination in the south. When the 'Peaks' were introduced between 15th August 1959 and 6th February 1960, they were all allocated to Camden shed 1B – on paper – but in reality they were loaned to Derby shed so that 17A could evaluate the class prior to their acceptance into full service. In April 1960 they were released from the custody of 17A and sent to Camden or at least nine of them went because D8 was sent directly to Crewe North. Within days if 1B getting the bulk of the class they were split up further and Carlisle Upperby, Edge Hill and Longsight all got one or more to evaluate in express passenger service. *(below)* Setting out for the south with passenger stock, D7 remained on Camden's books and did so until 17th March 1962 when it was transferred to Toton with the rest of the class, their stint on the WCML well and truly over. The external condition of the diesel was typical of the period when Camden couldn't recruit cleaners and so everything looked the same – grubby! *SVMRC.*

(above) Helping out the local diesel shunter, Cl.5 No.45427 now performs a spot of shunting after propelling its train back into the goods loop. Something is pegged on the main-line and in order to assist the passage of express passenger trains, Carnforth was well equipped with at least two goods loops in both Up and Down directions. *(below)* Just as the sun is beginning to set, ex-works 'Jubilee' No.45643 RODNEY approaches Carnforth with a Down express in early September 1960. This Crewe North engine had already worked one and a quarter million miles in revenue service and there was still another six years to go before withdrawal! *Both SVMRC.*

(above) Heading an Up freight during the summer of 1962, Crewe North 'Jubilee' No.45553 CANADA is put into No.2 Loop at Carnforth to await the passage of an express passenger train. Over on the Down Goods Loop a Stanier Cl.8F with a coal train is waiting for a northbound express to clear a path. The tender coupled to No.45553 was its last but it was also its first Stanier tender; up until August 1958 this engine had been coupled to various Fowler tenders since new. *(below)* Passing the ballast wagons that seem to have been stabled in that siding for years, 'Patriot' No.45503 THE LEICESTERSHIRE REGT. approaches Carnforth with a Down express in August 1962. *SVMRC.*

Late morning in August 1962 and 'Duchess' No.46255 CITY OF HEREFORD coasts through Carnforth with the Up service of *THE CALEDONIAN*. With plenty of steam to spare – as usual – the Pacific has basically been taking it easy since Shap with little effort asked of the engine or fireman. By now a Kingmoor engine, the external condition of No.46255 looks rather murky and the working of this train was as a stand-in for a failed diesel. We shall follow the path of the Pacific southwards to the outskirts of Preston. *SVMRC.*

Having taken a quick sharp right turn at Flyde Junction just before Preston station – physically impossible but just imagine anyway – and positioned ourselves a little way to the north of Kirkham station we witness a double-headed excursion from Blackpool (Central) joining the line from Blackpool (North) and Fleetwood at Kirkham North junction in late June 1961. The motive power consisted Newton Heath 'Jubilee' No.45710 IRRESISTIBLE – now running with a Stanier tender coupled in February 1959 after twenty-three years from new coupled to various Fowler tenders (it was happening everywhere) – along with an unidentified Class 5. The load only consists of eight bogies which hardly required these two capable engines but line occupation on busy days saw many trains double-headed just to get engines where they were needed or out of the way where they weren't. The 'Jubilee' has recently visited works by its external appearance and indeed she had undergone a Heavy General during May – its last! The train had travelled via the coast line through St Annes and Lytham, the scenic route, and was possibly en route to Manchester (Victoria). *SVMRC.*

(opposite, top) Looking the other way, we have Crewe based EE Type 4 D304 en route to Blackpool (Central) with an eight coach train. The 'express' code is being shown by the discs but the 1P45 board is unknown to this compiler but there is every reason to believe it was one of the London trains heading for Blackpool (Central). Kirkham station was located in the distance beyond the road bridge. The goods yard on the right was still doing business – just! *SVMRC.*

(opposite, bottom) With eleven on – mainly BR Mk.1s note – Doncaster based Thompson B1 No.61122 joins the main-line after using the flying junction from the Marton line with a working for Sheffield. The date is August 1960 and this train has a number of options, route-wise, to get back home but the most obvious would have been Preston, Chorley, Manchester (Victoria), Miles Platting, Philips Park, Ashburys, Belle Vue, Romiley, Chinley, Dore, and Sheffield (Midland). Then there was the availability of using the former Lancashire & Yorkshire main-line via Littleborough and Summit tunnel, Todmorden, or via the East Lancashire line from Preston to Blackburn, Burnley, Copy Pit, Hebden Bridge, Mirfield, Barnsley, or ..... There were then, and still are a myriad of interesting routes available although not as many as in the 1960s. *SVMRC.*

(below) Polmadie 'Clan' No.72001 CLAN CAMERON negotiates Kirkham's North junction in August 1960. The Glasgow 'Clans' were no strangers to Blackpool during their lifetimes and would especially find favour with specials during 'Glasgow Fair' when the city went on holiday, Blackpool being a favourite destination of Glaswegians. Of the ten engines in the class, this particular engine was probably the most travelled – though not necessarily with the greatest mileage – having traversed the West Highland line to Fort William in preparation for working a special for the 'Clan Cameron Gathering' in June 1956 at Spean Bridge. It also spent time working on the East Coast main line from Haymarket shed shortly before this image was recorded. *SVMRC.*

(above) The south end of Preston station – the North Union section – where in August 1960 we have a pair of original 'Patriots' hogging the limelight beneath that magnificent signal gantry; Newton Heath's No.45515 CAERNARVON is shunting whilst preparing a train – most likely the rear half of the express from Glasgow brought in by D218 and which was split in platform 6. Over on the by-pass lines an Up van train is headed by Upperby's No.45507 ROYAL TANK CORPS. *(below)* No.45507 and its goods train get away once the express passenger trains have cleared off. *Both SVMRC.*

(top) Edge Hill EE Type 4 D218 whistles and thunders out of platform 6 with the Liverpool portion of an express from Glasgow in August 1960. This diesel-electric locomotive was about a year old but just look at the external condition of its flanks; it wasn't just steam which was suffering from the man-power crisis on BR. Initially allocated to Crewe North when new on 11th July 1959, D218 was transferred to Edge Hill – note the 8A painted on the buffer beam – on 8th August 1959. Shortly after this photograph was captured on film the big diesel was moved to Longsight where on 12th July 1961 it was named CARMANIA, albeit not in this disgraceful state. *(below)* A somewhat quieter moment in August 1960 sees locally based 'Jubilee' No.45582 CENTRAL PROVINCES marshalling a train alongside platform 6 at around midday. By the end of the year the Preston engine would have racked-up some 1.3 million miles in revenue service but just over one year after this image was recorded it moved on to Carnforth for its final year of operation before withdrawal in December 1962. Allocated to 24K when fire destroyed the roof at Preston engine shed on 28th June 1960, No.45582 was not amongst the thirteen casualties which included 'Scots' 'Jubilees' BR Standards and others. As luck would have it, she was in fact attending Crewe works and was about to receive a Light Intermediate repair. *Both SVMRC.*

A prial of 'Semi' images! Remaining at the south end of the station for the duration of our stay at Preston it is a busy August Saturday during the summer of 1961 as Camden 'Duchess' No.46246 CITY OF MANCHESTER departs with an Up express. *SVMRC*.

THE LAST YEARS OF STEAM ON THE LONDON MIDLAND REGION

This aspect of the engine reveals the all-welded tender – No.9749 – which was coupled to No.46246 during a Heavy Intermediate overhaul at Crewe from 16th May 1961. That tender remained with the Pacific until withdrawal and replaced the original de-streamlined tender – No.9809 – which had been coupled from new. *SVMRC.*

(above) Non-stop! With more than one camera recording its passage, another Camden 'Duchess' No.46240 CITY OF COVENTRY runs through Preston's platform 7 at about mid-day with the Up service of *THE CALEDONIAN* in August 1960. *(below)* Although the weather was often dull, the traffic situation at Preston was always lively. Also working along the line through platform 7, Springs Branch Super D No.49154 hauls this Up goods through Preston station in September 1960. Once the main-stay of heavy freight workings on the WCML, these formidable 0-8-0s were amongst the last L&NWR locomotives working for BR. At the time this image was recorded, Springs Branch shed still had twenty-one of the surviving 140-odd engines allocated. *Both SVMRC.*

(above) Just over twenty miles to go to its destination, an excursion from the West Midlands to Blackpool hauled by Rugby based Cl.5 No.45419 runs over the Down slow at Leyland in August 1961. In the distance is the Leyland vehicle factory which was mainly concerned at that time with building heavy goods vehicles and buses and was one of Britain's more successful automotive businesses but within a decade or so would become embroiled with Midlands-based car manufacturers, bad-management and communist-based unionism. *(below)* Crewe North 'Royal Scot' No.46166 LONDON RIFLE BRIGADE heads south through Farington Junction near Lostock Hall with an express in August 1961. *Both SVMRC.*

(above) Just as the 'Scot' clears the junction, an excursion from Leeds to Blackpool heads north towards Preston with Farnley Junction 'Jubilee' No.45708 RESOLUTION at the helm. The 4-6-0 had recently been fitted with AWS and a speedometer, the former enabling it to undertake journeys such as this. A long time occupant of Farnley Junction shed the 6P was no stranger to this part of the LMR. (below) One of the un-named 'Patriots' No.45510 from Carlisle Upperby makes haste through Farington Junction with a very long fitted van train in August 1961. The yards on the right are virtually empty of traffic, a reflection on BR's continuing reluctance to keep hold of the traffic it already had. In the right background can be seen the coaling plant at Lostock Hall motive power depot. *Both SVMRC.*

(above) Relegated now to parcels and van trains, the 'Princess Royal' class was not too far from 'throwing in the towel' as their former express passenger work was now in the hands of diesel locomotives. The date is August 1961 and Crewe North's No.46206 PRINCESS MARIE LOUISE looks slightly unkempt externally although mechanically sound with no steam leaks. These Pacifics were spending more and more time in store and during 1961 this engine only managed just over seventeen thousand miles in revenue earning service, less than a quarter of what it achieved three years previously. They still looked graceful even with all the filth clinging to them. Of the dozen 'Princesses' still operational in 1961, six went by the end of the year and the rest in 1962 including our subject here. *(below)* Another un-named 'Patriot' No.45513 from Carnforth, heads north with a fitted freight comprising insulated containers and vans. The white containers were most probably empty meat containers headed for Aberdeen. *Both SVMRC.*

(above) Un-named 'Patriot' No.45542 had been waiting for a northbound express to pass before leaving the Down goods spur near Farington junction in August 1960. The spur connected the Leyland vehicle factory to the main line and being a local engine allocated to Preston shed, No.45542 was seconded for shunting this day and the trailing load was destined for the yard on the Up side. Note the train of tracked armoured vehicles discreetly sheeted over! *(below)* It is interesting to see that this 'Duchess' No.46253 CITY OF ST ALBANS is making plenty of steam even though the trailing load with thirteen on is somewhat heavy. We are still near Leyland in August 1961. *Both SVMRC.*

(above) English Electric Type 4 D333 roars south over Farington Junction with the Up working of *THE ROYAL SCOT* in August 1961. By now this train, along with the other named trains linking Glasgow (Central) with London (Euston) – *MID-DAY SCOT* and *CALEDONIAN* – are down to just eight coaches in order to speed up the timings in the face of competition from British European Airways and their London-Glasgow shuttle service. Of course the trains had no hope in competing but only certain clientele could afford the air fares anyway. Those who used the train had to pre-book seat reservations as a 'no-standing' policy was brought in. The big diesel was one of those with split headcode boxes necessary to accommodate the central communication doors which were rarely used anyway as double-heading did not become normal practice in day-to-day operations on BR. *(below)* With an all-stations working from Blackburn to Wigan, Stanier Cl.4 tank No.42631 sticks to the 20 m.p.h. speed limit as it negotiates Farington Junction to gain the main line south in August 1961. *Both SVMRC.*

(above) Working a Blackpool (Central) to the West Riding train, Low Moor Cl.5 No.44694 and an unidentified sister head south to Euxton junction where they will leave the WCML and head east towards Bolton and Manchester. During summer weekends the passenger traffic using this junction was almost continuous with extra workings threading in between the normal traffic. *(below)* Heading south with a train of suburban stock in August 1960, Preston 'Jubilee' No.45633 ADEN brings the load from Lostock Hall over the junction at Farington onto the main line. The train of tracked armoured vehicles seen earlier with No.45542 is now safely tucked away behind the mineral wagons awaiting onward transit. *Both SVMRC.*

(top) Stored locomotives at Lostock Hall engine shed after the end of steam on British Railways. Stanier Class 5s dominate although 8Fs are also in profusion dumped on the area of the motive power depot where the long-removed coal stacks were once located. Someone has made an effort to empty some of the tenders before these locomotives went on sale but eventually the task became too much for the available staff and tenders were sent off to scrapyards with as much as seven tons of coal therein – the scrap merchants didn't really bother because such minerals could be resold or used. The scene was essentially a mini-Barry at the time but with a pure LMR 'feel' about it. Really it was quite surreal and it appeared that someone had shunted the engines into any available siding space and then simply gone home! (above) Another view of the 'dump' at Lostock Hall looking south-west! *Both PL/BLP.*

(opposite, top) We've arrived at Bolton (Trinity Street) just as a minor incident is unfolding. With the last vehicle – M11467M – of a passenger train not quite making the platform at Trinity Street station and straddling the junction at Bolton West, a family of intending alighting passengers have been left stranded in a compartment in this undated view of the junction circa 1958. What appears to be a porter is helping or at least abetting an adult female to make the climb down whilst two children have already – and easily no doubt – made the transition. Nowadays such an event would turn into a full-scale circus with emergency services attending and all railway movement stopped in the name of the H&SE. The four tracks going off to the right went north to Blackburn whilst the five tracks originating from beyond the lattice girder footbridge came from Horwich, Wigan and Preston. The footbridge spanned the whole junction and enabled pedestrians to walk from Trinity Street, alongside the roof of Bolton West signal box to John Street without any change of elevation. The tank engine – No.40105 – is one of Mr Stanier's version of the Fowler Class 3 and which was only slightly more successful. However, on this occasion the 2-6-2T was en route from Horwich works, after front-end attention, to Trafford Park its home shed since March 1957. *(opposite, bottom)* Entering Trinity Street station with a train from Blackburn to Manchester (Victoria) Stanier Cl.5 No.44948 has an interesting rake of vehicles in tow circa July 1960. On the right are the west-end carriage sidings – with a Cravens DMU about to enter the fray – which were dead level and therefore give an idea of the incline being negotiated by the Blackburn train. *Both PL/BLP.*

(below) Is this the train which brought uncertainty to a family wanting to leave the service at Trinity Street circa 1958? A double-headed working with just four carriages in tow and hauled by Cl.4 No.42299 and an unidentified BR Standard tender engine coasts beneath the footbridge already mentioned on the previous page. This view of the western side of the West junction at Trinity Street shows the fours tracks coming in from the west and the two west-to-east by-pass lines which made up the top of the wye configuration at Bolton West junction. Meanwhile, the mystery of the premature stopper remains! *SVMRC.*

A parting view of Bolton (Trinity Street) station in August 1960; Newton Heath 'Jubilee' No.45701 CONQUEROR was heading a Blackpool (Central) to Manchester (Victoria) excursion – C115 – loaded to seven non-corridor vehicles waiting patiently in the morning sunshine for the signalman to pull the lever off. Two points of note with this engine are (1) It was allocated to Newton Heath depot for the whole of its life – only a handful of other 'Jubilees' managing that one shed for life situation. (2) The tender coupled in this image is a Stanier type – No.10332 – which was acquired 6th February 1959; No.45701 was coupled to a Fowler tender – No.3945 – since new. And so to Manchester! *SVMRC*.

(above) Farnley Junction 'Crab' No.42774 drifts down Miles Platting bank and into Manchester (Victoria's) platform 11 with a train for Manchester (Exchange) and points west circa 1960. It appears that this 2-6-0 was deputising for a failed 'Jubilee' or even a 'Scot' on this train which originated in the North-East at Newcastle and was bound eventually for Liverpool (Lime Street). If they were in good condition and with a competent crew, these engines could just about handle these expresses when circumstances demanded. No.42774 had moved to Farnley Junction in June 1959 having spent its life serving numerous sheds on two of the former LMS Divisions - Midland, and Western. It was withdrawn in November 1963 at Manningham. *(below)* Two – Nos.52140 and 52279 – of the Miles Platting bank banking engines comprising a pair of 'A' Class 0-6-0s stabled awaiting business at Victoria station east end in 1960. *Both PL/BLP.*

(above) Not wholly recognisable from this aspect but this is Trafford Park Junction – the signal box was out of frame on the right – in August 1959. Derby based 4F No.43955 is making its way on shed to collect some decent coal to add to the rubbish in the tender bunker – note that neat cab extension. The flood-lighting tower belongs to a football club which has been finding it hard going in recent times, its noisy neighbour getting all the accolades after years of mixed fortunes. The same view today has in fact changed yet again as the industrial premises have disappeared whilst the football club has expanded its ground facilities. Trafford Park is still a name to be conjured with as regards railways but nowadays it's more to do with freight than locomotives. And now we move on to London Road station. *PL/BLP. (below)* With the amount of natural light bathing the terminus, it must a summer's morning as *THE MANCUNIAN* express awaits departure from the old platform 3 at Manchester (London Road) circa 1956. This was before the catenary for the 25kV electrification was erected, Type 4 diesels were still on the drawing board and the rebuilding of the station had started. Note the two carriage boards indicating the name of the train and the cities served, along with their relevant Coat-of-Arms. For its non-stop run the express departed Manchester at around 0930 (departure varied with the decades but only by minutes) with a 1320 arrival in London. The return working left Euston at 1750 with arrival in Manchester at 2140 with a stop at Wilmslow to set down. One of the early LMS innovations, the express was inaugurated in 1927 but stopped running in 1966 when the new all-electric timetable was introduced. *SVMRC.*

(above) 'Britannia' No.70044 EARL HAIG has the Up working of *THE MANCUNIAN* at London Road station in March 1957. It's damp but not raining but it is March! No.70044 was a Longsight engine, basically had been since new and was therefore a regular on this express duty. Note the catenary masts marking the eastern limit of the Manchester South Junction & Altrincham electrification from Oxford Road station. *(below)* Another rather murky day at Manchester (London Road) circa 1958; Longsight 'Royal Scot' No.46158 THE LOYAL REGIMENT heading the Up working of *THE MANCUNIAN* adds to the gloom. The first vehicle of the train has double-headboards note. The station is in the throes of modernisation including massive change involving platform replacement, renewal and change of the track layout, and electrification! Not a lot really if you say it fast. The task would take a couple of years to complete and was being carried out during a period when BR was rather cash-strapped whereby certain jobs took longer to do than planned. In the meantime this departure would take us as far as Slade Lane, Longsight where the express would take the line to Styal whilst we continue along the main line. *Both SVMRC.*

(*above*) However, before we leave Manchester (London Road) let's take a look at some of the work proceeding during 1958. It is a typical murky autumn day in the city centre with fog or even smog threatening to descend. We are looking along the line towards Oxford Road station with two bridges immediately apparent, the first being the one spanning Fairfield Street and the second – with catenary still in place – spanning London Road itself. All of this area of the station was completed demolished and a new bridge created which today carries platforms 13 and 14. The terminal platforms are just to the right beyond the cast-iron columns. The line here used to carry the MSJ&A electrified railway which was now terminated at Oxford Road station in order to allow the Manchester-Crewe 25kV electrification to reach Oxford Road station. There was, as the saying goes, much work to be done! (*below*) About five miles from London Road we enter the leafy suburbs of Stockport and its first station after crossing the county border from Lancashire into Cheshire. 'Jubilee' No.45638 ZANZIBAR runs through Heaton Chapel & Heaton Moor station on the Down fast with an express from Cardiff for Manchester (London Road) in 1957. Note the colour-light signalling which had recently been completed – March 1955 – between Levenshulme and Heaton Norris. Prior to the 1955 modernisation of the signalling, a small signal box was located on a brick plinth between the Up and Down fast lines just about where the tender is passing. Known by signalmen as 'the rat trap' or 'the rabbit hutch' the box was rather close to the action. The post-war neglect of these stations was still evident but the forthcoming Manchester-Crewe electrification scheme would change the look of the whole line with station rebuilding and bridge renewal taking place along the route. *SVMRC.*

(left) With its home shed forming the background, Crewe North 'Duchess' No.46225 DUCHESS OF GLOUCESTER is coaled up and ready for the labours to come whilst waiting for a Down express in May 1959.

(below) A view looking south from the footbridge at the north end of Crewe station in late May 1959 revealed this gathering of two of Stanier's celebrated Pacifics. Polmadie based 'Princess Royal' No.46210 LADY PATRICIA and 'Princess Coronation' No.46221 QUEEN ELIZABETH, of Crewe North. No.46210 had just arrived with a working from Scotland and was standing on No.2 through road waiting for a path to Crewe North engine shed. No.46221 was awaiting a Down express which she would take north to Carlisle; the headboard gives the clue. *Both SVMRC.*

(above) 'Princess Royal' No.46210 LADY PATRICIA makes her way to Crewe North shed past the crowds of 'platform-enders' who watch her progress. To some of them she was quite a rare bird now or had been since her transfer to Polmadie in July 1958. Applied during a Heavy General overhaul carried out at Crewe in March 1958, No.46210 had been wearing a wrong-facing BR crest on the right side of her tender but that was put right during a Heavy Intermediate overhaul which took place towards the end of the summer timetable. *(below)* What the 'Duchess' and her pair of coaches were waiting for. The first leg of *THE MID-DAY SCOT* was hauled from London by Edge Hill 'Princess Royal' No.46209 PRINCESS BEATRICE........*SVMRC*.

(above) Yet another 'Princess Royal' heads for the shed. No.46209 leaves THE MID-DAY SCOT in platform No.2 – note that first item of rolling stock – to await the arrival of No.46221 and her short addition to the train. No.46209 had just had a long spell in works receiving Casual Light repair which was to make good accident damage. Meanwhile, a clutch of 'spotters' watch her stately progress to the shed. (below) An undated photograph of three ex-works locomotives entering Crewe North shed with all of them in steam circa March 1959. The trio consisted of BR Standard Cl.2 No.78043 from Bank Hall which would probably get a temporary job as station pilot whilst running-in. The Cl.2 is coupled to 'Royal Scot' No.46133 THE GREEN HOWARDS which had completed a Heavy General at Crewe and was being taken to North shed from 5B after the usual ex-works routine of taking locomotives departing from works to South shed for lighting-up. Kentish Town was the home shed of the 'Scot' so its running

in would be conducted from North shed and which would eventually entail a working to London where No.46133 can then make its way back to the Midland Division main line. The 'Duchess' is No.46257 CITY OF SALFORD which had also completed a Heavy General but on the day before the 4-6-0. No.46257 was an Upperby engine and would eventually get back to Carlisle after a series of running-in trips from North shed, the first of which was hauling this little load from 5B. Note the masts being erected for the forthcoming electrification scheme. *Both SVMRC.*

(top) By using a route branching off the WCML at Stafford and travelling south via Wolverhampton we are able to reach Bescot yard comfortably and have a quick look at the myriad of lines spreading out from the north end of Bescot especially. However, we need to look at some serious metalwork before we go anywhere beyond the yard limits. With an express for Wolverhampton (High Level) 'Duchess' No.46240 CITY OF COVENTRY stops at Bescot station whilst being diverted from Birmingham (New Street) via Soho Road and Handsworth Wood on Friday 2nd August 1963. There are some delighted young gentlemen on the platform getting a closer look than they normally would. *(above)* This is Super D No.49407 with its 21B shed plate missing. The engine appears to be engaged in trying to reach its home shed on the west side of the railway here and is about to proceed tender first onto the spur leading off on the right. In the distance Bescot station sits behind the footbridge which linked the motive power depot to the staff car-park. It is worth giving this image another good looking at because nowadays it is nearly unrecognisable especially the scene to the left which now has the M6 Motorway soaring overhead on those concrete stilts which took the road southwards to its junction with the M5 – the scene of many hours of jams for regular users of the motorway in these parts. That lattice-girder bridge on the left looks infinitely better than the station bridge but I don't think it lasted many more years. *Both PL/BLP.*

(above) Observed from the footbridge seen in the previous view, Ivatt Cl.2 No.46456 hauls a short freight off in the direction of Dudley Port on Friday 2nd August 1963. *(below)* Super D No.49361 departs from Bescot tender first and heads towards Walsall on Friday 9th August 1963. *Both PL/BLP.*

(above) Heading back in a north-westerly direction we visit the engine shed which supplied Wolverhampton's former LMS side with its motive power – Bushbury. Stanier 'Crab' No.42965 was stabled at its home shed Bushbury – 21C then – on Friday 9th August 1963. It arrived here during the previous March and Bushbury was to prove to be its final shed where it was withdrawn in August 1964. Since being put into traffic at Leeds Holbeck in January 1934, this engine served at no less than sixteen different depots. *(below)* CITY OF COVENTRY rests on Bushbury engine shed on 9th August 1963, a week after we first spotted the 'Duchess' at Bescot on the Midlands express; it looks as though she has become a regular for the Friday working. *Both PL/BLP.*

(opposite top) Leaping across the West Midlands we had deviated off the WCML once more but this time we have taken the eastern loop from Rugby to Northampton: Standing at platform 1 – the Up platform – resident Cl.5 No.45292 heads a local passenger service at Northampton (Castle) during the summer of 1960. The photographer is standing on island platform 6 looking south. This station was built in 1880 on the site of what remained of Northampton Castle (built 1084 by Simon de Senlis), the majority of the ruined walls of which were demolished to make way for the railway station; but a section known as a postern gate was preserved and moved to a new site on the boundary of the station precinct – even in 1880 public pressure could achieve such results. The station opened for business on 1st December 1881 and had three through platforms: No.1, with 6 and 7 forming the island on the Down side. There were five terminal platforms or bays: Nos.2, 3, 4 and 5 on the Up side and another bay on the Down side at the northern end of platform 6. This view also reveals Northampton No.2 signal box located just south of the bridge at the end of terminal platform 4; No.1 signal box was behind the camera. No.2 was the largest of four boxes and had 118 levers. In April 1966 – by now this was the only railway station in town – Castle station lost its suffix and became simply Northampton but as part of the rebuilding for the electrification to Euston, the two-storey Victorian station building with its Italianate style design was demolished and replaced by what was described at the time as three cow sheds built in steel, glass and concrete; clean airy but quite ugly compared to what had gone before. The station was totally redeveloped in 2013-15 at a cost of £20 million, its appearance now being even more unrecognisable from these images. *PL/BLP.*

NORTHAMPTON – A brief visit!

(above) Looking north we see No.45292 as seen from beneath the St James' Road/Black Lion Hill road bridge during that summer of 1960. Steam motive power was banned from Northampton from 27th September 1965 when the current of the newly erected electrification was switched on for business. As part of the 2015 station rebuilding the station's previous name of Northampton Castle was to be restored but this was reported to cost in excess of £200,000 to bring to fruition and it was left in abeyance. *PL/BLP*.

(above) Back to the main line and continuing our journey south we meet DP2 working a Down express at Tring on Saturday 11th May 1963. This English Electric Type 4 prototype was loaned to the LMR for evaluation in May 1962 and worked mainly from Camden depot. Unlike its noisy predecessor DP1, with its two Napier Deltic engines, this locomotive had one EE 16-cylinder 16CSVT engine which set the two prototypes apart: DP2 went on to win an order from BR (LMR) for fifty-one locomotives which later became BR Class 50. One of the 2,700 h.p. engines in the production batch of locomotives originally powered DP2; this event took place because an accident on the ECML brought about DP2's premature end which saw the locomotive scrapped at Vulcan Foundry but its prime mover was salvaged. *(below)* Immediately DP2 and its train had cleared the location, Willesden based Stanier 8F No.48665 came into view with a short ballast train probably being positioned for Sunday's engineering works on the WCML. *Both PL/BLP.*

(above) Having gone forward in time to 20th July 1963 we have also moved a little further south and have reached the northern portals of Northchurch tunnels – 29 miles and 12 chains from Euston. The three bores are each 347 yards long, not the longest on the WCML but long enough to give the Civil Engineer a headache with the advancing electrification, the masts of which stand defiantly at the entrances. Bursting out of the double bore tunnel, Patricroft 'Jubilee' No.45563 AUSTRALIA was something of a rarity around these parts during BR days so the local spotters' would be made-up to see its presence even with that coat of filth as it worked an excursion northwards. (below) Toton's Stanier 8F No.48125 works a coal train southwards to London on that same July day in 1963 and is approaching the Northchurch tunnels. *PL/BLP.*

Two views at Watford Junction in 1959 *(top)* Bushbury 'Jubilee' No.45741 LEINSTER approaches the station with an express from Wolverhampton. Watford engine shed presents a smart face to the main line with white-washed walls and a flower bed along the west wall; note the lack of ash piles, etc. about the yard. *(above)* A Down afternoon express roars through platform 6 with rebuilt 'Patriot' No.45535 SIR HERBERT WALKER, K.C.B. in charge. The stock is certainly rocking about; note the second vehicle especially – anyone for tea? *Both PL/BLP.*

(above) Less than sixteen miles from Euston now as yet another Toton 8F – No.48186 – is caught passing the water softener for Bushey troughs on 14th September 1963 with the inevitable coal train in tow. The 2-8-0 is one of the balanced – starred – members of the class which enabled them to run faster with these coal trains much like the Annesley to Woodford coal trains known as 'Runners' on the GC main line. Note no masts here yet but lots of coal bound for Metropolis! *PL/BLP*. (below) Heading a late afternoon northbound express; 'Royal Scot' No.46125 ROYAL ARMY SERVICE CORPS dips into Bushey water troughs during the summer of 1958. *SVMRC*.

(above) Before its transfer to the Southern Region in December 1959 BR Standard Cl.4 No.80066 was allocated to Watford shed from new in the summer of 1953 along with sisters Nos.80064, 80065, 80067, and 80068; Nos.80034 to 80038 were also on Watford's books from new in 1952. Here in 1958 our subject dares to dip into the troughs whilst working an evening commuter service and being less than two miles from home. However the Watford engines worked to Tring, Northampton and even Rugby so this service could continue northwards after the Watford Junction stop. Whilst all of the class were fitted with internal pipework to distribute water picked up from troughs, only the London Midland allocated members of the class were fitted with bi-directional scoops. *SVMRC. (below)* The Down service of *THE SHAMROCK* left London at around 1645 with an arrival time in Liverpool being around 2100. This September 1959 view of the train has Edge Hill 'Scot' No.46155 THE LANCER taking water from the troughs at Bushey; the next chance to take water will be some forty miles distant at Castlethorpe, north of Wolverton. *PL/BLP.*

(above) As the evening shadows grow longer in the late summer of 1959, an 8F – No.48262 – from Crewe South brings a mixed fitted freight into London but isn't bothering to pick-up any water. This view reveals which troughs were being used the most with the Down fast as the most popular!

(below) 'Royal Scot' No.46132 THE KING'S REGIMENT LIVERPOOL heading the Up service of *THE MANXMAN* has a last refill of the tender tank on Bushey troughs circa 1960. This train ran from 1927 to 1966 with only WW2 interrupting its service during that time. *Both SVMRC.*

Just before its transfer from Camden to Preston, 'Royal Scot' No.46168 THE GIRL GUIDE runs over Bushey troughs with an Up express in the late summer of 1959. Water troughs were expensive to maintain, the destructive nature of torrents of water was forever causing PW problems and as can be seen here drainage was constant. Winter of course brought with it a new set of problems to be overcome. *SVMRC.*

(above) A Euston-Watford electric service consisting two London District standard three-car sets passes a young spotter overlooking the water troughs at Bushey on a summer evening circa 1959. The 630v DC 3rd and 4th rail electric units were built to a BR standard design and were essentially all Second class accommodation seating 256 passengers in each three-car unit: Motor Open Brake Second; Trailer Second; Open Brake Second; the fleet consisted some fifty-seven cars of each type. *SVMRC. (below)* Empties going back to the coalfields! Near Bushey troughs, Willesden 8F No.48665 – again – heads north with a train of empty 16-ton mineral wagons on the morning of Saturday 27th July 1963. *PL/BLP*.

(above) Skirting the troughs! On 27th July 1963 a six-car Watford line unit heads into London past the water troughs whilst a photographer rewinds his camera alongside the ballast box. Nowadays such an incident as letting a non-railway worker being so close to the trains would not be allowed, conspicuity clothing or not, but BR once trusted photographers enough to give them line-side passes to indulge their hobby. Common sense prevailed in every way. *(below).* Dipping the scoop in Bushey troughs! Working a Down express, Camden based 'Duchess' No.46240 CITY OF COVENTRY picks up a few thousand gallons of water to keep the tender topped-up on 27th July 1963. The photographer seen at a distance in the previous image is now keeping a safe distance from the water spray. *Both PL/BLP.*

(above) Willesden 'Britannia' No.70034 THOMAS HARDY obviously had no requirement for extra water so didn't lower the scoop whilst working this Up express through Bushey cutting on 27th July 1963. *(below)* Another empty coal train plies north along the Down slow on Saturday 27th July 1963. This is one of the Stonebridge Park power station special trains – fourteen bogies and a brake van – which at this time hauled coal supplied from Calverton Colliery a relatively new pit north of Nottingham. The self-discharging bogie wagons were of 40-ton capacity and had lower side discharge doors. Introduced by the LMS in 1929, the wagons were operational until 1967 when the power station was closed. Some thirty wagons consisting of four different versions were constructed for the traffic and these were numbered 189301 to 189330. Originally marshalled into ten-wagon trains, they latterly ran as two longer trains allowing wagons to be stopped for overhaul or repair. The purpose of Stonebridge Park PS was to generate power for the 630v DC electric trains plying between Euston and Watford, beside the Watford extension of the Bakerloo London Underground line. The route taken by these coal trains saw them leave Toton yard and travel south via Market Harborough, and Northampton to reach the WCML. *Both PL/BLP.*

(above) Crewe North Cl.5 No.44678 marks its passage through Hatch End on 28th September 1963 with some reasonable pollution for the period. Running on the Down fast with a fully fitted van train, the 4-6-0 would be in Basford Hall yard in about four hours traffic permitting. *(below)* Willesden engine shed on Saturday 21st July 1962 with visitors to the fore! The Toton 8F, No.48125, on the right was not really a stranger to this place, 18A sending half a dozen of their eight-coupled charges down to this part of London every day with coal trains. However, slightly nearer the camera is V2 No.60871 which is bereft a 34A shed plate and which came from just a few miles to the south and east but it was another BR Region. No matter which region of BR was highlighted at this time most if not all locomotives had that coating of filth and the air of neglect. *Both PL/BLP*.

(above) The engine named after the man who started the LMS motive power revolution. 'Duchess' No.46256 SIR WILLIAM A. STANIER F.R.S. looking rather neglected at Willesden shed in 1961. The Pacific had transferred from Camden to Crewe during the previous year and the start of 1961 saw the engine resident in the works which built it having a two-month long Light Intermediate overhaul. That event appears not to have taken place looking at the external condition of the engine but No.46256 had put in a lot of miles in 1961 and not a lot of shed time. Things did get better for this magnificent machine but only temporarily – *see* page 81 – because in October 1964 she was condemned and then scrapped. *(below)* Back on the main line and heading north through the junction at Willesden, 'Britannia' No.70019 LIGHTNING of Crewe North has a rake of green Southern Region carriages in tow as it comes off the line from west London. The working – 1M36 – is an unknown express but we have a date of 16th August 1964 – a Sunday – which might help. In the left background the new Willesden electric traction depot is taking shape. *Both PL/BLP*.

(top) Before it all went-to-the-wall! 'Duchess' No.46245 CITY OF LONDON runs through Kensall Green over the last four miles of its journey south with this express on 1st June 1963. *(above)* Rebuilt 'Patriot' No.45534 E TOOTAL BROADHURST about to enter the 317 yards long Kensall Green tunnel on 21st July 1963 with a Down passenger train. *Both PL/BLP*.

(above) A Crewe North 'Duchess' on 13th July 1964 in the new 'filthy black' livery which most of the 'into-1964' survivors carried through their final months. This is No.46228 DUCHESS OF RUTLAND with a fitted freight bound for Camden goods depot. (below) Heading for Willesden, Class 4 2-6-4T No.42102 hauls empty Post Office vehicles through Kensall Green on 13th July 1964. *Both PL/BLP*.

(above) The Up service of *THE CALEDONIAN* with that unique 5ft wide headboard, runs through Camden on the final leg of its journey from Glasgow during the summer of 1959. 'Duchess' No.46242 CITY OF GLASGOW is the motive power and the Pacifics' nearly empty tender tells the story of its 401-mile slog with this somewhat lightweight train, at least by WCML standards. Introduced on Monday 17th June 1957 for the summer timetable, this express stopped only at Carlisle where just two minutes was allowed within the six hours and forty minute schedule. The seating arrangement provided for 84 first and 120 second class passengers. During the seven years it plied the WCML the express saw numerous changes with the initial daily service – 0830 Up from Glasgow in the morning and 1510 afternoon arrival at Euston, the Down being a 1615 departure from London with late evening arrival at Glasgow (Central). For a short period during the summer of 1958 the service was increased to two daily departures each way – morning and afternoon. By 1959 the work on the electrification scheme of the WCML south of Crewe started to affect speeds and the winter of that year saw the Glasgow to London schedule increased to seven hours fifteen minutes. The last service was run as a named express on Friday 4th September 1964. *(below)* Another Euston-bound express rounds the curve from Primrose Hill tunnels during the summer of 1959 with 'Royal Scot' No.46101 ROYAL SCOTS GREY in charge. This recent Camden acquisition was transferred from Crewe North during the previous June. The 7P ended its days at the end of the summer timetable in August 1963 working semi-fasts over former Great Central metals from Nottingham (Victoria) to London (Marylebone). *Both SVMRC.*

(above) Early afternoon at Camden shed during the summer of 1959 with plenty of activity positioning locomotives ready for their next workings. Amongst the steam locomotives identified are 'Jubilee' No.45638 ZANZIBAR, 'Scot' No.46157 THE ROYAL ARTILLERYMAN, and fresh off *THE MERSEYSIDE EXPRESS*, 'Princess Royal' No.46211 QUEEN MAUD, the latter waiting for the turntable which was about to be vacated by another 'Scot' No.46108 SEAFORTH HIGHLANDER from Longsight with the *EMPRESS VOYAGER* headboard. One of the new English Electric Type 4 diesels D213 looks on whilst being refuelled from the temporary fuelling point consisting two four-wheel tank wagons. The nearest two locomotives have been serviced and are now about to reverse into the shed to join the various queues for Down workings. Just out of sight to the right was 'Jubilee' No.45664 NELSON which was a rare visitor from Millhouses. Note that various shades of filth appear to be the livery of the day. *(below)* Time marches on and just as QUEEN MAUD is about to be positioned beneath the coaling plant, a Manchester express thunders by on the Down fast with Longsight's Rebuilt Patriot No.45540 SIR ROBERT TURNBULL at the helm. *Both SVMRC.*

Camden shed during a busy period. Everything happened to a sequence. It worked like a dream for nearly thirty years! *SVMRC.*

(above) Taking the Watford lines with an empty stock working, un-rebuilt and un-named Patriot No.45549 runs over a very useful diversionary route to get beyond the congested lines on this side of Primrose Hill during busy periods. The Warrington Dallam based 6P was listed to be named R.A.M.C. but the union never did take place. (below) During the summer of 1961 the Down service of THE CALEDONIAN departs London in the late afternoon behind Upperby 'Duchess' No.46226 DUCHESS OF NORFOLK. The average speed of THE CALEDONIAN for the first summer of service in 1957 had a respectable 60.2 m.p.h. for both trains. The headboard initially was a painted steel version but that was replaced by a cast alloy example with raised letters and a raised rim. The twin shields represented St Andrew and St George and that basically remained the headboard design throughout the life of the train. When diesel locomotives took over in 1962 a smaller headboard some three feet wide was created in wood and painted. For the record, our 'Duchess' here, No.46242 worked the inaugural Down service in June 1957; the locomotive working the Up service is alas unknown to this compiler. As a show of continuing improvements in express travel, the LMR worked THE CALEDONIAN through the winter months too. The motive power depot appears a little quieter now as main-line diesel locomotives have settled into sharing the WCML expresses with steam. Three Type 4s and a Type 2 are on view here. Note that the rudimentary diesel fuelling facility using tank wagons has been abolished and a proper fuelling pad – out of sight – has been set up to cater for the growing fleet of diesels. *Both SVMRC.*

(above) Straddled above the Watford lines, the photographer captures 'Princess Royal' No.46204 PRINCESS LOUISE bringing an afternoon express through the maze of lines which from Primrose Hill tunnels dipped and dived and burrowed all the way into Euston station. *(below)* Late morning and a splendid summers' day in 1959 sees *THE MANCUNIAN* running through Camden for an on-time arrival at Euston with Longsight 'Royal Scot' No.46140 THE KING'S ROYAL RIFLE CORPS. Many passenger trains travelling via Crewe from Manchester at this time were electric hauled as far as Crewe where steam or diesel took over but this long-standing non-stop express from Manchester kept the same motive power all the way from London Road (nee Piccadilly) to Euston until the electrification to Euston was complete; it then ceased to exist having been superseded by a faster morning train catering for businessmen. By the end of this 1959 summer season's timetable, No.46140 would transfer to Kentish Town depot (14B) to work a completely new route for the 7P. *Both SVMRC.*

(*above*) We saw her earlier queuing on Camden shed; here is the train which brought 'Jubilee' No.45638 ZANZIBAR into London in August 1959. (*below*) Earlier in the day an Upperby based 'Scot' has steam to spare as it gets an express rolling north. Note the gauging men on the Watford electrified lines. *Both SVMRC.*

Double-heading! *(above)* Having virtually finished its run from Wolverhampton (High Level), *THE MIDLANDER* drifts through Camden with ample motive power in the shape of Class 5 No.44687 and an unidentified short-named 'Jubilee' in the summer of 1959. The Longsight Cl.5 was one of two (44686 was the other) in the 800+ class equipped with Caprotti valve gear, Skefko roller bearings, double chimney, and a high running plate. Introduced in 1951 they were the culmination of BR experimentation with Stanier's wonderful Class 5 4-6-0s from which the BR Standard Cl.5 was developed. *(below)* A northbound afternoon express is headed by a Rose Grove Cl.5 and an unidentified 'Royal Scot' passing Camden in summer 1959. No.44948 was not really required to help the 7P with its heavy load, it was merely hitching a ride back home after an unbalanced working which brought it to London. To keep line occupation down to a minimum over the extremely busy WCML, it was necessary to double-head engines with train engines rather than sending them off 'light'. *Both SVMRC.*

(above) One of the much maligned Fowler Cl.3 2-6-2Ts – motor-fitted No.40010 – uses the Watford line to haul e.c.s. away from Euston to Willesden in 1959. There are at least ten bogies in the train but the Cl.3 appears to be handling the load without fuss. Willesden had twenty-one of these engine allocated at this time but many of them were soon to be placed into store whilst others were to be transferred; our subject was amongst the latter group and was moved to Nuneaton in May 1960 but, like a bad penny, returned to Willesden in June 1961 only to be withdrawn the following month. *(below)* Seemingly racing with a Watford line electric unit, 'Brit' No.70047 – the un-named one! – has steam to spare as it runs through Camden with the Down service of *THE SHAMROCK*. Departing Euston at 1645, this train got into Liverpool (Lime Street) at 2105 with plenty of time for prospective passengers to catch the overnight sailing to Ireland. *Both SVMRC.*

(above) Summer 1960! *THE CALEDONIAN* again with an Up service winding through Camden with 'Duchess' No.46244 KING GEORGE VI in charge. *(below)* Willesden had a whole host of steam locomotives – mainly tank engines – engaged in the movement of empty carriage stock into and out of Euston station. This Fowler Cl.4 – No.42360 – had been transferred to 1A in October 1957 but in February 1958 it went to Longsight only to return to London just a few weeks later. However in June 1958 it ventured north again to 9A for a longer stint there. It came back from Manchester in September and remained at Willesden until withdrawn in August 1961 approximately a year after this image was recorded showing the 2-6-4T catching its breath after its labours climbing Camden bank with this rake of stock from an Up express working. Besides the Cl.4s, Willesden had the Cl.3 versions to call upon; perhaps the most unusual tank engines of recent times were the pair of Thompson L1s acquired from Neasden during the summer of 1958 whilst this Cl.4 and another of its kind were in Manchester. Note the electrification warning plates on the tank ends; these were a reminder of its short time spent at Longsight where the forthcoming 25kV electrification was already being used. The shed is busy processing the afternoon cavalcade of diesel and steam locomotives ex-Euston. In the background it is nice to see Camden goods depot was employing three of 1B's 350 h.p. 0-6-0DE shunters. Ernest Marples had a lot to answer for! *Both SVMRC.*

(above) It wasn't all Pacifics and namers hauling the expresses out of Euston! This Birmingham (New Street) express has Monument Lane's Stanier Class 5 No.45308 in charge on a summer's day in 1960. 'Royal Scot' No.46125 3RD CARABINIER has just finished the servicing procedure and will soon reverse onto the shed to await its next job. *(below)* An unusual choice of motive power for empty stock working, summer 1960! Ivatt Cl.2 No.46472 was a new arrival at Willesden in May after seven years on the North Eastern Region, a year at Rugby and less than six months at Chester. It was becoming something of a headache for the authorities to find suitable work for these engines. *Both SVMRC.*

That's right they came in from the left, crossed over the stabling roads onto the 70ft turntable where a ninety degrees anti-clockwise turn put them onto the coaling road; through the coaling plant and onto the ash pits on the south end of the shed where fires and ash pans were cleaned. Tenders filled with water, repeat the journey along the road at the east side of the shed but continue past the turntable road, and reverse onto the shed to stable awaiting further duties. That was basically the sequence that steam locomotives went through at this particular motive power depot which with its restricted space but fairly large and very active allocation. Camden was one of the first sheds chosen by the LMS to modernise the Motive Power Department to maximise efficiency. Of course the mechanical coaling and ash plants were also provided, as was the 70ft turntable. It didn't come cheaply but it certainly made a difference to locomotive servicing and over the next few years following the implementation of the scheme in 1935 fewer locomotives were required to work the same amount of traffic. *SVMRC.*

It was a busy turntable at Camden, not just turning locomotives but it was an integral part of the servicing procedure whereby steam locomotives had to use it in order to take up their next duties out of Euston or Camden goods yard. Here Bushbury Cl.5 No.45439 is about to take advantage of a clear run to the coaler watched by diesels and other 4-6-0s. Note the cowling around the wagon hoist on the coaling plant. That addition was fitted to try to alleviate coal dust nuisance affecting the local residencies which backed onto the shed yard. British Railways and Camden council were regular adversaries in court, be it smoke nuisance, blowing-off safety valves or good-old dirt! *SVMRC*.

Meanwhile on the main line! Even though Longsight had a small fleet of Type 4 diesels to use by summer 1960, *THE MANCUNIAN* was still worked by the depot's reliable 7P 4-6-0s as here with 'Rebuilt Patriot' No.45530 SIR FRANK REE doing the honours and drifting though Camden bank ready for the descent of Camden bank; due Euston 1320. *SVMRC.*

The Last Years of Steam on the London Midland Region

(top) Back on shed we are in amongst the diesels! An immaculate SIR WILLIAM A. STANIER F.R.S. stands defiant on the last day of May 1963. The cleaning was all down to shed staff at Crewe and Camden. *(centre)* On the same day, and not looking anything like as assured as No.46256, sister No.46252 CITY OF LEICESTER was dumped on a siding at the southern end of the shed yard, its shed plate removed and no doubt now worn by one of the diesel interlopers. The very next day this 'Princess Coronation' was withdrawn, just three months and a week before Camden shed closed its doors to steam. *(above)* This is Camden remember! So, we are going to see LM Pacifics quite a lot. Having visited the coaling plant Upperby 'Duchess' No.46237 CITY OF BRISTOL is having its fire cleaned on Saturday 13th July 1963. The Fowler tender in part view – No.4508 – belonged to Crewe North 'Jubilee' No.45704 LEVIATHAN. *All PL/BLP.*

(above) The Empire was contracting! 'Jubilee' No.45580 BURMA is connected to the turntable vacuum tractor on that same July Saturday ready for a quick anti-clockwise 90 degrees swing. This engine was one of Warrington Dallam's handful of recently acquired 6Ps and had been at the Lancashire shed just three weeks when this image was recorded. On the right is one of Camden's 350 h.p. 0-6-0DE shunters – D3848 – which was one of half a dozen of the class employed at 1B at that time. *(below)* Beneath the coaler, Crewe North 'Brit' No.70025 WESTERN STAR is about to receive about six tons of coal from the overhead bunker. It will be quality stuff, Camden being one of the lucky few sheds on the LMR to be supplied with decent steaming coal. The irony perhaps was that the Standard locomotive classes were equipped with fireboxes which could burn the worst coal mined in the UK – apparently. *Both PL/BLP*.

(above) Another view of CITY OF BRISTOL going through the servicing procedure on 13th July 1963 and being got ready to work back home. None of the LM Pacifics were looking their best by this time – 46256 apart – and this lady was becoming distinctly grubby; still she worked for another year and three months unlike No.46252 in the left background which was still awaiting haulage north to the works at Crewe for breaking-up! (below) Camden has now finally been given over to the diesels and on Sunday 8th September 1963 CITY OF LEICESTER is almost ready for the journey north. As already mentioned, the shed plate has been removed but everything else is still attached to the rather grimy Pacific. Note the chimney covering and the greased motion; it was rumoured at the time that certain LM Pacifics might find work on the Southern Region. However, No.46252 was due for a heavy overhaul and boiler change therefore the chance of survival for this engine was very slim. Indeed later that same month nineteen years old No.46252 entered the locomotive works at Crewe and became one of sixteen 'Duchess's' cut up that year at the place of their birth! Both PL/BLP.

(above) Whilst working an Up express in 1960 'Duchess' No.46253 CITY OF ST ALBANS makes for a nice study, coasting beneath the bridge which carried Regent's Park Road over the railway at Camden,. Note the empty tender, and the rather filthy external condition of the Crewe North based Pacific. The time is 1715. *(below)* The reason for the empty tender; photographed a few moments earlier, No.46253 was working *THE ROYAL SCOT*. Note the Mk.1 coaching stock now in use for this train at that time. *Both SVMRC.*

(above) Crewe North 'Jubilee' No.45684 JUTLAND sets out for home from Camden Goods depot with a fitted freight on an August evening in 1960. *SVMRC. (below)* And so to Camden bank! Making it look easy! No.46240 breasts the bank with a Down express on 2ⁿᵈ August 1963. *PL/BLP*.

(top) You can see why the signal box was called Euston Carriage Sidings. On an unknown date but post June 1959 when 'Jubilee' No.45578 UNITED PROVINCES was fitted with AWS and September 1959 when the 6P transferred from Crewe to Edge Hill, the 4-6-0 clambers up Camden bank with a mixed bag of stock. *SVMRC. (above)* As Willesden based Stanier Cl.5 No.45374 backs down to the terminus, an unidentifled Fowler Cl.3 2-6-2T, also from Willesden, has its work cut-out hauling twelve vehicles of empty stock up the bank in 1959. *Both SVMRC.*

(right) A view of some of the track employed around Euston Carriage Sidings box in summer 1959 with Rugby Class 5 No.44771 ready for some work. These 4-6-0s – on what was regarded as 'local' workings – were serviced at Willesden shed, with only the 'elite' engines off the long distance expresses being serviced at Camden.
(below) After working into Euston with a train from Northampton in 1959, Cl.5 No.45331 was put to work taking empty stock out of the terminus and is seen during the seemingly endless busy periods when trains or light engines were on the move constantly. Both SVMRC.

Another morning departure for the north! After its 0935 departure from Euston with twelve on – the optimum load – 'Royal Scot' No.46160 QUEEN VICTORIA'S RIFLEMAN starts the climb up to Camden in late August 1959 with *THE COMET*, due Manchester 1320. This Longsight Scot had been at 9A since LMS days but in mid-September next it switched allegiance to the old Midland Division with a transfer to Kentish Town depot. *SVMRC.*

It's all gone quiet! Well nearly! Bushbury 'Jubilee' No.45737 ATLAS eases a Down Wolverhampton service past Euston Carriage Sidings box in late summer 1959. *SVMRC.*

(*Page 90*) 'Royal Scot' No.46170 BRITISH LEGION drifts down the bank to Euston in 1959 to take up an express working. This was the one-off 'Scot' rebuilt from No.6399 FURY in 1935 and which had a boiler – No.2 in the LMS scheme – which was also a one-off! This predicament meant No.46170 spent more time in works than any other 'Scot' with five months typically being required for a Heavy General as against four to six weeks for other members of the class. Note the ex-LMS 3F 0-6-0Ts doing a lot of the pilot work around the station and its approaches. (*left*) On the same day Edge Hill 'Princess Royal' No.46208 PRINCESS HELENA VICTORIA is captured backing down to the terminus ready to work the Down service of *THE MANXMAN* to Liverpool (Lime Street). *Both SVMRC.*

(above) One of Watford's 1952 batch of BR Standard Cl.4s – No.80034 – is about to use the underpass to cross to the west side of the running lines during the late summer of 1959. Note the locomotive at the rear of the train which is still attached! *(below)* Making a song-and-dance of it all! It is now approaching 1000 hrs and a few minutes after the Standard 4 has crept northwards, less than splendid 'Duchess' No.46255 CITY OF HEREFORD passes on the Down main with the northbound *ROYAL SCOT*. Meanwhile three of the four locomotives waiting on the east side of the main line are blowing off as if trying to make the noise of the express. *Both SVMRC.*

(top) Brand new! EE Type 4 D224 is on the bank in August 1959. New to Camden shed on 15th August 1959 – the only new one 1B got from the initial LMR batch D210-D236 – the diesel is attached to the end of a rake of coaching stock being taken down to Euston along one of the dedicated Watford lines. D224 was being tested as to its accelerating prowess especially on the bank with a heavy load. Although the bottom section of the image was cut-off, it does not detract from the subject. *SVMRC. (above)* Settled-in, for now! Crewe-based EE Type 4 D336 tops Camden bank with a Down express on 2nd August 1963. These 133-ton monsters took the WCML express workings by storm – noisily might be more appropriate – when they virtually ousted steam but the timetable was never altered to allow them to reveal their full potential. Could they have accelerated the timings? Probably as they could sustain continuous full power for longer periods; what they did allow was to give quicker turnaround times with minimum servicing; a switch-on-and-go facility if you like. In 1966 their short reign on the WCML expresses was over and done. That year saw the introduction of electric locomotives which did radically transform express timings. Nowadays multiple units have slashed even more off those timings so that the 1950s four-hour schedules with steam haulage between London and Manchester for instance has been taken below the two-hour mark. Sixty years has seen a revolution but what will the next 60 years bring? *PL/BLP.*

(top) Consummate ease! An evening arrival with 'Duchess' No.46239 CITY OF CHESTER in charge brings another WCML express to the end of its journey. The year is 1958 and Euston is looking tired wearing its usual grimy post-war drab. Rebuilding of the station and electrification are some years off and before then steam will be eliminated in favour of diesel-electric locomotives and they in turn will be expelled by electric traction. However, the arrivals will still come into the east side of the station and departures will generally leave from the west side of the terminus. Some things rarely change. *(above)* We're missing a headlamp! Rugby Cl.5 No.44863 and an unrecorded 'Scot' arrive at Euston's old platform 3 with an Up express circa 1959. Note the attire of the young spotters' thronging the platform end: polished shoes, jackets, etc., with not an anorak or a pair of jeans in sight! *Both PL/BLP.*

(above) Crewe North 'Royal Scot' No.46128 THE LOVAT SCOUTS bringing an Up express into Euston amidst mixed interest with the spotters' in 1959. Except for a couple of loans to Holbeck lasting only a few months in the 1940s, this engine spent the whole of its life working the WCML between Glasgow and London. *(below)* We don't know what time *THE SHAMROCK* terminated at Euston's platform 1 but it was due at 1215. The clock states 1254 which tells us some thirty-nine minutes have elapsed since booked arrival time and one would think that by now 'Princess Royal' No.46204 PRINCESS LOUISE would have been released to back up to Camden shed. The day is somewhere around 1959 when this Edge Hill engine became a regular on the 0805 service out of Lime Street. *Both PL/BLP*.

(above) During its final year as a Longsight engine, 'Royal Scot' No.46111 ROYAL FUSILIER waits at the head of a Manchester express at a dilapidated Euston in May 1959. *(below)* We finish off with this image of a Down departure leaving Euston circa 1960 with 'Patriot' No.45548 LYTHAM ST ANNES showing off its steam generating capability. This is what the north end of the terminus looked like before 1966. Note the ‡ower bed and the part-time gardener enjoying a fag whilst tending a nice linear horticultural display. Welcome to Euston! *Both PL/BLP.*